THAT'S THE JOB FOR ME!

I'M GOING TO BE A
WRITER!

BY MICHOU FRANCO

Gareth Stevens
PUBLISHING

Please visit our website, www.garethstevens.com. For a free color catalog of all our high-quality books, call toll free 1-800-542-2595 or fax 1-877-542-2596.

Library of Congress Cataloging-in-Publication Data

Names: Franco, Michou, author.
Title: I'm going to be a writer! / Michou Franco.
Description: Buffalo : Gareth Stevens Publishing, 2025. | Series: That's
  the job for me! | Includes index.
Identifiers: LCCN 2023038192 (print) | LCCN 2023038193 (ebook) | ISBN
  9781538293386 (library binding) | ISBN 9781538293379 (paperback) | ISBN
  9781538293393 (ebook)
Subjects: LCSH: Authorship–Juvenile literature.
Classification: LCC PN159 .F665 2025 (print) | LCC PN159 (ebook) | DDC
  808.02–dc23/eng/20230927
LC record available at https://lccn.loc.gov/2023038192
LC ebook record available at https://lccn.loc.gov/2023038193

Published in 2025 by
Gareth Stevens Publishing
2544 Clinton Street
Buffalo, NY 14224

Copyright © 2025 Gareth Stevens Publishing

Designer: Claire Zimmermann
Editor: Therese Shea

Photo credits: Cover, pp. 1 metamorworks/Shutterstock.com; Series Art (background) Salmanalfa/
Shutterstock.com; p. 5 diignat/Shutterstock.com; pp. 7, 19 Evgeny Atamanenko/Shutterstock.com; p. 9 fizkes/
Shutterstock.com; p. 11 Rawpixel.com/Shutterstock.com; p. 13 BeeBright/Shutterstock.com; p. 15 zefart/
Shutterstock.com; p. 17 Gorodenkoff/Shutterstock.com; p. 21 Elena Medoks/Shutterstock.com.

CPSIA compliance information: Batch #CS25GS: For further information contact Gareth Stevens, New York,
New York at 1-800-542-2595.

Find us on

CONTENTS

Boldface words appear in the glossary.

Writer in Training

I love to read all kinds of books. My favorite kinds are fairy tales, **poetry**, and funny stories. I love to write too. And I *really* love to share what I write. So, I'm going to be a writer!

Write Now!

You have to wait until you're older to do many jobs. You have to be a certain age. Or you have to wait until you finish school. But writers can be any age! They just need to know how to read and write.

What to Write

Writers choose to write fiction or nonfiction. Fiction is about characters and events that a writer imagines. They aren't real. Fairy tales and **novels** are fiction. Nonfiction tells facts about real people and events. History and **biographies** are nonfiction.

The Audience

Writers think about their audience. The audience is the people who read a book or other writing. For example, children are an audience. To write for children, writers use words and ideas children will understand. Many adults like to read children's books too!

Editing

Most writing has errors, or mistakes, at first. That's why writers edit. Editing means getting writing ready for others to read. Editing might mean cutting some words. It might mean fixing **punctuation**. It might mean changing something that doesn't sound right.

your success
after a while yu
track of
too
use a
rejection
and

Publishing

Some writers work for publishing companies. A publishing company prepares, produces, and sells books and other writings. The company pays the writer for their work. Some writers work for **magazines**, newspapers, and internet sites. And some writers publish and sell their own work.

College

Some people go to **college** to study a kind of writing. **Creative** writing students may learn how to write poetry, novels, **scripts**, and more. **Journalism** students learn how to write news stories. Other college students learn to write for businesses.

A Different Way

Some famous writers never went to college. They read a lot, though. They learned from other writers. Some writers do other jobs while they work on their writing. It may take them many years to finish a book or other written work.

Just Write!

I'm learning a lot in school about writing. For example, punctuation helps me **communicate** my ideas clearly. I'm practicing the skills I need to be a good writer. I'm writing stories for my friends too. I'll be a famous writer someday!

biography: The story of someone's life written by another person.

college: A school after high school.

communicate: To share ideas and feelings.

creative: Showing or having the skill of coming up with new ideas or making new creations.

journalism: Collecting, writing, and editing news.

magazine: A type of thin book with a paper cover that contains writings and pictures that is often published weekly or monthly.

novel: A long written story often about fictional characters and events.

poetry: Writing in verse that sometimes tells a story.

punctuation: Marks, such as periods and commas, used to make the meaning of a piece of writing clear.

script: A written plan for a show.

FOR MORE INFORMATION

BOOKS

Bradley, Doug. *Writer*. New York, NY: PowerKids Press, 2023.

Raffa-Mulligan, Teena. *You Can Be a Writer!* Perth, Australia: Sea Song Publications, 2020.

WEBSITES

How to Write a Great Story in 5 Steps
www.grammarly.com/blog/how-to-write-a-story/
Learn more about the parts of a fiction story here.

Types of Writers
www.masterclass.com/articles/types-of-writers
There are many kinds of writers. Read about 14 kinds on this site.

INDEX

leveled reader
social studies

THAT'S THE JOB FOR ME!

THAT'S THE JOB FOR ME!
I'M GOING TO BE A
BALLET DANCER!
leveled reader

THAT'S THE JOB FOR ME!
I'M GOING TO BE A
DOCTOR!
leveled reader

THAT'S THE JOB FOR ME!
I'M GOING TO BE AN
ENGINEER!
leveled reader

THAT'S THE JOB FOR ME!
I'M GOING TO BE A
PILOT!
leveled reader

THAT'S THE JOB FOR ME!
I'M GOING TO BE A
TEACHER!
leveled reader

THAT'S THE JOB FOR ME!
I'M GOING TO BE A
WRITER!
leveled reader

ISBN: 9781538293379

9 781538 293379